HOW PRINTING HELPS US

By Sybil Anderson McCabe

Director of Instruction
Napa County Schools
Napa, California

Pictures–Lucy and
John Hawkinson

BENEFIC PRESS · CHICAGO

Publishing Division of Beckley-Cardy Company

Atlanta   **Dallas**   **Long Beach**   **Portland**

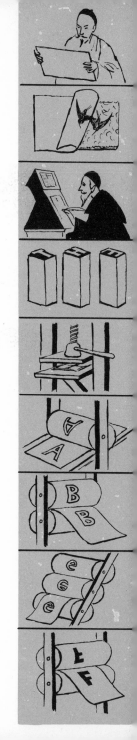

Supplementary

Social Studies Program

How Series

HOW HOSPITALS HELP US
HOW SCHOOLS HELP US
HOW WE CELEBRATE OUR SPRING HOLIDAYS
HOW WE GET OUR MAIL
HOW WEATHER AFFECTS US
HOW FAMILIES LIVE TOGETHER
HOW DOCTORS HELP US

HOW AIRPLANES HELP US
HOW WE CELEBRATE OUR FALL HOLIDAYS
HOW WE GET OUR CLOTHING
HOW WE TRAVEL ON WATER
HOW FOODS ARE PRESERVED
HOW WE GET OUR DAIRY FOODS

HOW WE GET OUR CLOTH
HOW WE GET OUR SHELTER
HOW WE TRAVEL ON LAND
HOW PEOPLE LIVE IN THE BIG CITY
HOW COMMUNICATION HELPS US
HOW PRINTING HELPS US

Basic Concepts Series

HOW MAPS AND GLOBES HELP US
HOW PEOPLE LIVE IN THE MIDDLE EAST
HOW PEOPLE LIVE IN JAPAN
HOW PEOPLE LIVE IN AFRICA
HOW THE NEW WORLD WAS DISCOVERED
HOW DOCUMENTS PRESERVE FREEDOM
HOW PEOPLE LIVE IN CENTRAL AMERICA
HOW SCHOOLS AID DEMOCRACY

Photographs furnished by:

W. F. Hall Printing Company
Inland Lithograph Company
Rand McNally and Company
LST Typography

Library of Congress
Number 64-19186

CONTENTS

SHARING IDEAS

Long, long ago no one knew how to read or write. Yet, the people wanted a way to share their stories and ideas with others.

Some early people cut pictures into rocks. The pictures told a story they wanted to share.

It was slow, hard work to cut a picture story into rock.   The rock could not be carried from one place to another.   Only those people who passed by the rock would see the story.

5

How did clay tablets help?

Some early people learned to make tablets of clay. They put clay into a frame. They cut pictures into the clay while it was wet.

They baked the clay to make it hard.

Many clay tablets were needed to tell a story.

After people learned to use letters and words, they did not need many tablets to tell one story. They wrote more kinds of stories and ideas on their clay tablets.

The clay tablets could be carried from one place to another. More people could share the stories and ideas.

Many times the clay tablets broke. People needed something that would last a longer time.

7

How was the first paper made?

The early Egyptian people made a kind of paper from a special plant that came from their part of the world. They used a kind of picture writing on their paper. They could keep rolls of their writings for a long time.

Papyrus plant

Papyrus paper

Parchment

Many years later the Egyptian people learned to make a kind of paper from animal skins. This kind of paper would last a very long time. People in other parts of the world used this kind of paper, too.

The Chinese were the first to make paper something like the paper of today. They made the paper from the wood of a special kind of tree.

Wood of the mulberry tree

How was the first printing done?

The first kind of printing was done by the Chinese people. They cut pictures into wood blocks. The pictures stood up from the wood.

They spread ink over the raised part of the picture. When they pressed the block onto paper, the picture was printed.

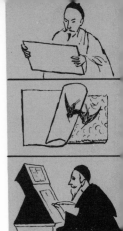

The Chinese used block printing to print many pictures. They tried printing letters, too. But that idea did not work well. Chinese writing has too many letters.

People in other parts of the world learned to make paper and block prints from the Chinese. They put block-print pictures in their books, but all the writing was done by hand.

Not many books could be made in this way. Most people did not learn to read or write because they had no books.

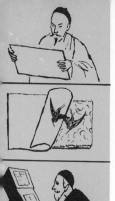

THE FIRST PRESS

One day a man named Gutenberg had an idea. He tried cutting just one letter at a time on a small piece of metal.

After working a long time, he had many letters. Each letter stood up from the metal.

Mr. Gutenberg put some of
his letters together to make words.
He put the words into a kind of tray.

Over the letters he spread a
special kind of ink that he had made.

The man had also made a large press. It was
made of wood. He put the tray of letters on the press.
Then he placed a piece of paper over the letters.

He pressed the paper against the letters.

Mr. Gutenberg took the paper off the press. The letters and words were clearly printed on the paper. His idea had worked. He had made a printing press.

Soon Mr. Gutenberg was using his letters and his press to print books. When he was finished printing one book, he put all the letters away. He could use the same letters over and over again.

Other men, too, were soon using the idea of the printing press. They printed books and other things.

More and more people learned to read. They could read about other people's ideas. They could read stories for fun.

GETTING READY TO PRINT

If Mr. Gutenberg could see some of the great presses today, he would be very much surprised.

The presses of today do not look at all like the first ones that were made. Yet, the ideas of many years ago are still used in printing today.

What work is done before
a book is printed?

Many workers are needed
before a book is printed.

One worker must write
the book.

Another worker must go over
the writing to see that everything
is right. He plans where the
words and pictures will go.

Layout
editor

18

This worker
makes pictures
for the book.

Artist

Photographer

This worker
gets pictures
for the book, too.

Book
editor

The story and pictures are
put together the way they
will be in the book.

Hand-set type

Type-setting machine

The book must be set in type. Some of the big type will be set by hand.

Most of the type will be set by this machine. Each letter has a key. The worker presses the keys. Thin pieces of metal with raised letters and words come from the machine. The words come one after the other as they will be in the book. There is one line of type on each piece of metal.

The pieces of metal go into the tray.

Soon the tray is full. Another worker puts the tray of type on a small press. He prints a copy of the type.

The copy is read to see that the type is right. Type that is not right must be set again.

Proof press

Proofreader

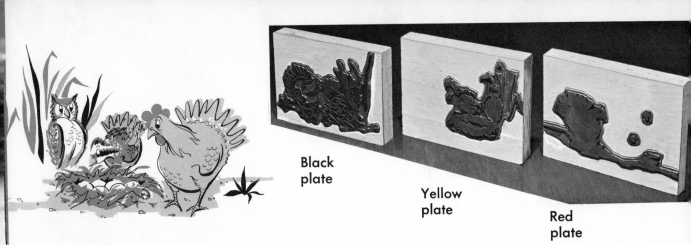

Black
plate

Yellow
plate

Red
plate

While workers are getting the type ready, other workers are getting the pictures ready for the press. Workers make metal plates like the pictures. If the pictures are colored, each color has its own plate. The plates are put on wood blocks.

Page lock-up

The metal type and the plates for the pictures are put together as they will look on the pages of the book.

Now the plates that will
go on the press can
be made. The pictures
and the type for each
page are put onto one
metal plate.

Some press plates are flat.
Other press plates are curved.
Each color has its own press plate.

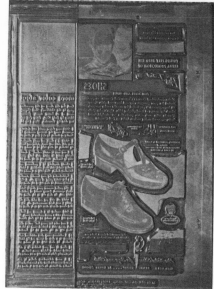

Flat press plate
(black only)

Curved press plates
(four colors)

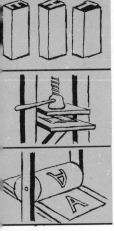

ON THE PRESS

After the plates are made, the book is ready for the press. If the plates are flat, they are put on this kind of press.

Rollers are used to put ink on the plate.

One big roller presses the paper against the type. The paper passes all the way around this roller.

The plate moves from the inking rollers to the printing roller each time a sheet is printed.

Flat-bed letterpress press

Impression cylinder

Inking rollers

Press plates

If the press plates are curved, they are put on a press that has a printing roller.

Another roller presses the paper against the printing roller. Other rollers put ink on the printing roller. All the rollers go round and round when the press is running.

Rotary letterpress press

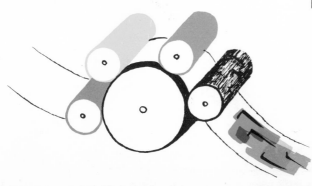

If color is used, there is a printing roller for each color.

The papers are folded
and cut into pages.

The pages are
sewed together.

The cover is
put on last.

MORE PRESSES

Other important ways to print are also used today. One way that is being used more and more is offset printing. Special presses are made to do offset printing.

The words and pictures for offset printing are put on clear sheets. These clear sheets are film.

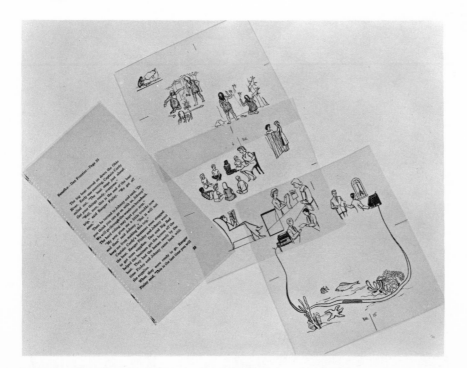

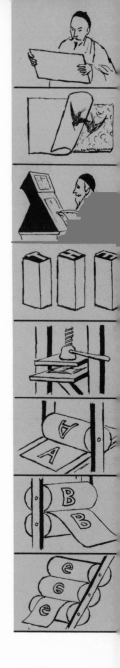

How is an offset press plate made?

A worker puts together the film for the type and the pictures as they will look on each page. He puts many pages together.

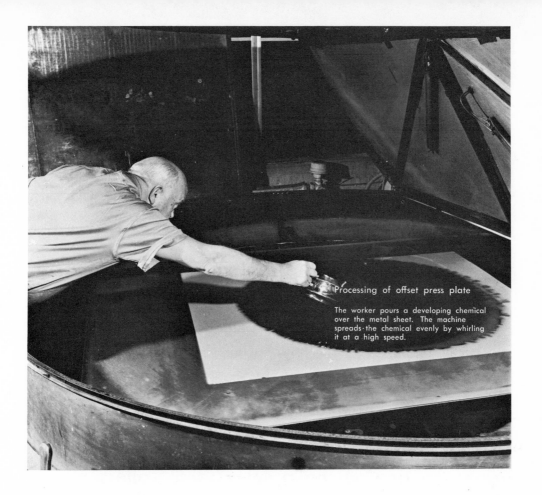

Processing of offset press plate

The worker pours a developing chemical over the metal sheet. The machine spreads·the chemical evenly by whirling it at a high speed.

This worker is making the thin metal printing plate that will go on the offset press. His work will put the words and pictures on the film onto the plate.

The type and the pictures do not stand up from an offset plate. It is not easy to see them.

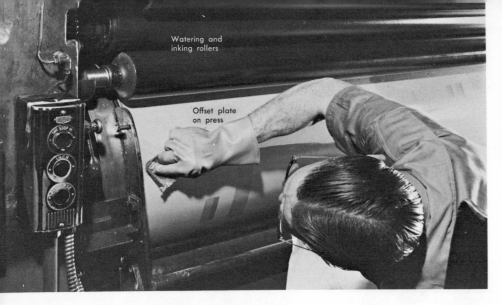

Watering and inking rollers

Offset plate on press

Cleaning of plate on offset press

How does an offset press work?

An offset press has a number of rollers. The offset plate goes on one of the rollers. Some rollers put water and ink on the printing plate. Ink sticks to the part of the plate to be printed. Water sticks to the rest of the plate. The water keeps the ink from spreading.

Another roller on the press is covered with rubber. One other roller presses the paper against the rubber.

When the press is running, the ink from the printing plate sticks to the rubber roller.

The words and pictures are printed from the rubber roller onto the paper. The paper is pushed against the rubber roller by another roller.

On an offset press, there is a set of rollers for each color that is to be printed.

The press in this picture has two sets of rollers. It can print two colors.

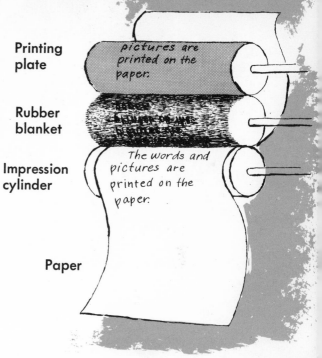

Printing plate

Rubber blanket

Impression cylinder

pictures are printed on the paper.

The words and pictures are printed on the paper.

Paper

Two-color offset press

Watering and inking rollers

Plate

Rubber blanket

Impression cylinder (not visible in this photograph)

Roll of paper
being fed to press

Roll to be used
when top roll is
empty

Web-fed press

On some big presses, the paper goes into the press
from big rollers. These presses cut the paper after
it is printed.

Printed press sheets

Printed press sheets

Four-color offset press

On other presses, the paper is cut before it goes into the press. Many pages are printed on each big sheet. These sheets will be folded and cut into book pages.

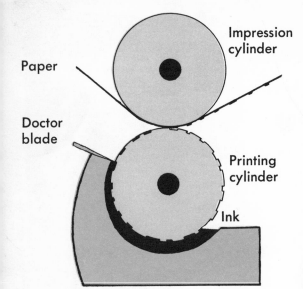

Paper

Impression cylinder

Doctor blade

Printing cylinder

Ink

Another kind of printing plate is made by cutting down into the metal. The words and the pictures are like little wells in the printing plate. The plate is a large metal roller.

Printing cylinder for gravure press

When the press is running, the little wells are full of ink. The ink from the wells prints the words and pictures on the paper.

This kind of printing is good to use when many pictures are to be printed.

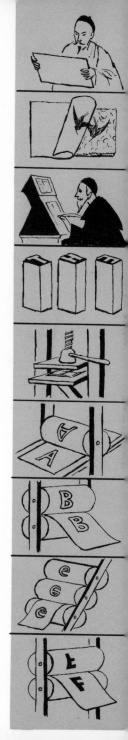

MANY KINDS OF PRINTED MATTER

A great many copies of a book are printed on one run of the press. The printers keep the plates. The book can be printed again if more copies are needed.

Children in all parts of the country can use the same books.

Many books are used in schools. But there are many, many other kinds of books.

Some books are for small children.

Some books are for older children.

We can learn many
ideas from books.

Other books have stories
just for fun.

There are books that
tell how to do things.
There are many, many
kinds of books about
people, animals, and places.

Newspapers, too, are printed on printing presses. All over the world, many newspapers are printed each day. Some newspapers are large. Some are small.

It takes many workers for a large newspaper. Some workers get news and pictures for the newspaper.

Other workers get the news ready to print.

Current
events

Sports

What kinds of things does
a newspaper tell?

A newspaper prints
something for every reader.
There is important news
from other parts of the
world. There is news from
all parts of the country.

Some parts of the newspaper have special
kinds of news.

Newspapers have stories, pictures, and special ideas.

Fashions, recipes, child care, home arts

Part of the newspaper is fun for children.

Comics

Other parts of the newspaper tell about things people want or need.

Advertisements

What can people read in magazines?

Magazines are another important kind of printed matter. They are printed on big presses, too. Some magazines are printed many times a year.
Others are not.

Some magazines are for children. The magazines may have stories for fun. They may give ideas. They may tell how to make things.

Some magazines
have mostly stories.
Others have stories
and pictures about
just one thing.

Some magazines have
ideas to help people in
their work.

What are some other kinds of printing?

Printing can be found in many places.
Each kind of printing has a special use.

All of this printing is on paper.

There is printing on things that are not paper, too.
These things need special presses. Each is printed in
a special way.

PRINTING HELPS PEOPLE

Printing helps people in many ways. Today we can read books and papers that were printed many years ago. We can learn about the people of many years ago.

A long time from now, people may read books that were printed today. They may learn about the people of today from the books they read.

Printing helps bring
people together from all
over the world. Sometimes
people want to help other
people they have read about.

Printing helps people learn
many of the things they
need to know. Printing is
important to people
everywhere.

Vocabulary

The total vocabulary of this book is 225 words, excluding labels. Of these, 14 are third-grade words, 8 are above third-grade, and 203 are below third-grade level. Third-grade words are listed below in roman type. Words above third-grade are listed in italic type. The number after each word indicates the page on which it first appears.

Chinese 9
curved 23

Ideas 5
important 27
ink 10

roller 24

Egyptian 8

machine 20
magazines 42
metal 12

Sharing 5
sheets 27
special 8

newspapers 39

film 27
folded 26
frame 6

pressed 10
printing 10

tablets 6
tray 13
type 20